CW00421020

# Francis Frith's
# Hastings & Bexhill

*Photographic Memories*

# Francis Frith's
# Hastings & Bexhill

John Bainbridge

FRITH
BOOK Co

Paperback edition first published in the United Kingdom in 2000 by
Frith Book Company Ltd

British Library Cataloguing in Publication Data

Francis Frith's Hastings & Bexhill
John Bainbridge
ISBN 1-85937-131-0

Frith Book Company Ltd
Frith's Barn, Teffont,
Salisbury, Wiltshire SP3 5QP
Tel: +44 (0) 1722 716 376
Email: info@frithbook.co.uk
www.frithbook.co.uk


Printed and bound in Great Britain

*Front Cover:* Hastings, The Esplanade 1925  77976

AS WITH ANY HISTORICAL DATABASE THE FRITH ARCHIVE IS CONSTANTLY BEING CORRECTED AND IMPROVED
AND THE PUBLISHERS WOULD WELCOME INFORMATION ON OMISSIONS OR INACCURACIES

# Contents

# Francis Frith: *Victorian Pioneer*

**FRANCIS FRITH**, Victorian founder of the world-famous photographic archive, was a complex and multi-talented man. A devout Quaker and a highly successful Victorian businessman, he was both philosophic by nature and pioneering in outlook.

By 1855 Francis Frith had already established a wholesale grocery business in Liverpool, and sold it for the astonishing sum of £200,000, which is the equivalent today of over £15,000,000. Now a multi-millionaire, he was able to indulge his passion for travel. As a child he had pored over travel books written by early explorers, and his fancy and imagination had been stirred by family holidays to the sublime mountain regions of Wales and Scotland. 'What a land of spirit-stirring and enriching scenes and places!' he had written. He was to return to these scenes of grandeur in later years to 'recapture the thousands of vivid and tender memories', but with a different purpose. Now in his thirties, and captivated by the new science of photography, Frith set out on a series of pioneering journeys to the Nile regions that occupied him from 1856 until 1860.

## Intrigue and Adventure

He took with him on his travels a specially-designed wicker carriage that acted as both dark-room and sleeping chamber. These far-flung journeys were packed with intrigue and adventure. In his life story, written when he was sixty-three, Frith tells of being held captive by bandits, and of fighting 'an awful midnight battle to the very point of surrender with a deadly pack of hungry, wild dogs'. Sporting flowing Arab costume, Frith arrived at Akaba by camel seventy years before Lawrence, where he encountered 'desert princes and rival sheikhs, blazing with jewel-hilted swords'.

During these extraordinary adventures he was assiduously exploring the desert regions bordering the Nile and patiently recording the antiquities and peoples with his camera. He was the first photographer to venture beyond the sixth cataract. Africa was still the mysterious 'Dark Continent', and Stanley and Livingstone's historic meeting was a decade into the future. The conditions for picture taking confound belief. He laboured for hours in his wicker dark-room in the sweltering heat of the desert, while the volatile chemicals fizzed dangerously in their trays. Often he was forced to work in remote tombs and caves where conditions were cooler. Back in London he exhibited his photographs and was 'rapturously cheered' by members of the Royal Society. His reputation as a photographer was made overnight. An eminent modern historian has likened their impact on the population of the time to that on our own generation of the first photographs taken on the surface of the moon.

## Venture of a Life-Time

Characteristically, Frith quickly spotted the opportunity to create a new business as a specialist publisher of photographs. He lived in an era of immense and sometimes violent change. For the poor in the early part of Victoria's reign work was a drudge and the hours long, and people had precious little free time to enjoy themselves. Most had no transport other than a cart or gig at their disposal, and had not travelled far beyond the

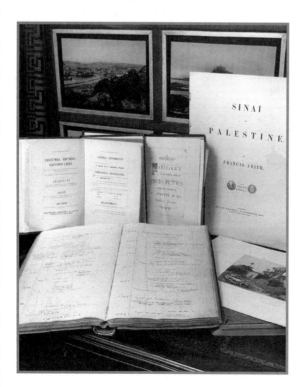

boundaries of their own town or village. However, by the 1870s, the railways had threaded their way across the country, and Bank Holidays and half-day Saturdays had been made obligatory by Act of Parliament. All of a sudden the ordinary working man and his family were able to enjoy days out and see a little more of the world.

With characteristic business acumen, Francis Frith foresaw that these new tourists would enjoy having souvenirs to commemorate their days out. In 1860 he married Mary Ann Rosling and set out with the intention of photographing every city, town and village in Britain. For the next thirty years he travelled the country by train and by pony and trap, producing fine photographs of seaside resorts and beauty spots that were keenly bought by millions of Victorians. These prints were painstakingly pasted into family albums and pored over during the dark nights of winter, rekindling precious memories of summer excursions.

## The Rise of Frith & Co

Frith's studio was soon supplying retail shops all over the country. To meet the demand he gathered about him a small team of photographers, and published the work of independent artist-photographers of the calibre of Roger Fenton and Francis Bedford. In order to gain some understanding of the scale of Frith's business one only has to look at the catalogue issued by Frith & Co in 1886: it runs to some 670 pages, listing not only many thousands of views of the British Isles but also many photographs of most European countries, and China, Japan, the USA and

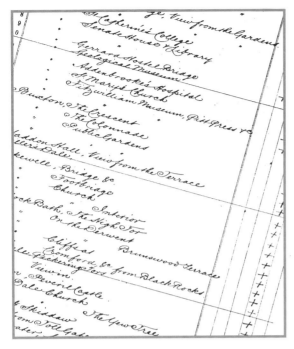

Canada – note the sample page shown above from the hand-written *Frith & Co* ledgers detailing pictures taken. By 1890 Frith had created the greatest specialist photographic publishing company in the world, with over 2,000 outlets – more than the combined number that Boots and WH Smith have today! The picture on the right shows the *Frith & Co* display board at Ingleton in the Yorkshire Dales. Beautifully constructed with mahogany frame and gilt inserts, it could display up to a dozen local scenes.

## Postcard Bonanza

The ever-popular holiday postcard we know today took many years to develop. In 1870 the Post Office issued the first plain cards, with a pre-printed stamp on one face. In 1894 they allowed other publishers' cards to be sent through the mail with an attached adhesive halfpenny stamp. Demand grew rapidly, and in 1895 a new size of postcard was permitted called the court card, but there was little room for illustration. In 1899, a year after Frith's death, a new card measuring 5.5 x 3.5 inches became the standard format, but it was not until 1902 that the divided back came into being, with address and message on one face and a full-size illustration on the other. *Frith & Co* were in the vanguard of postcard development, and Frith's sons Eustace and Cyril continued their father's monumental task, expanding the number of views offered to the public and recording more and more places in Britain, as the coasts and countryside were opened up to mass travel.

Francis Frith died in 1898 at his villa in Cannes, his great project still growing. The archive he created continued in business for another seventy years. By 1970 it contained over a third of a million pictures of 7,000 cities, towns and villages. The massive photographic record Frith has left to us stands as a living monument to a special and very remarkable man.

# Frith's Archive: *A Unique Legacy*

**FRANCIS FRITH'S** legacy to us today is of immense significance and value, for the magnificent archive of evocative photographs he created provides a unique record of change in 7,000 cities, towns and villages throughout Britain over a century and more. Frith and his fellow studio photographers revisited locations many times down the years to update their views, compiling for us an enthralling and colourful pageant of British life and character.

We tend to think of Frith's sepia views of Britain as nostalgic, for most of us use them to conjure up memories of places in our own lives with which we have family associations. It often makes us forget that to Francis Frith they were records of daily life as it was actually being lived in the cities, towns and villages of his day. The Victorian age was one of great and often bewildering change for ordinary people, and though the pictures evoke an impression of slower times, life was as busy and hectic as it is today.

We are fortunate that Frith was a photographer of the people, dedicated to recording the minutiae of everyday life. For it is this sheer wealth of visual data, the painstaking chronicle of changes in dress, transport, street layouts, buildings, housing, engineering and landscape that captivates us so much today. His remarkable images offer us a powerful link with the past and with the lives of our ancestors.

## Today's Technology

Computers have now made it possible for Frith's many thousands of images to be accessed almost instantly. In the Frith archive today, each photograph is carefully 'digitised' then stored on a CD Rom. Frith archivists can locate a single photograph amongst thousands within seconds. Views can be catalogued and sorted under a variety of categories of place and content to the immediate benefit of researchers.

Inexpensive reference prints can be created for them at the touch of a mouse button, and a wide range of books and other printed materials assembled and published for a wider, more general readership - in the next twelve months over a hundred Frith local history titles will be published! The day-to-day workings of the archive are very different from how they were in Francis Frith's time: imagine the herculean task of sorting through eleven tons of glass negatives as Frith had to do to locate a particular

**See Frith at www. frithbook.co.uk**

sequence of pictures! Yet the archive still prides itself on maintaining the same high standards of excellence laid down by Francis Frith, including the painstaking cataloguing and indexing of every view.

It is curious to reflect on how the internet now allows researchers in America and elsewhere greater instant access to the archive than Frith himself ever enjoyed. Many thousands of individual views can be called up on screen within seconds on one of the Frith internet sites, enabling people living continents away to revisit the streets of their ancestral home town, or view places in Britain where they have enjoyed holidays. Many overseas researchers welcome the chance to view special theme selections, such as transport, sports, costume and ancient monuments.

We are certain that Francis Frith would have heartily approved of these modern developments in imaging techniques, for he himself was always working at the very limits of Victorian photographic technology.

## The Value of the Archive Today

Because of the benefits brought by the computer, Frith's images are increasingly studied by social historians, by researchers into genealogy and ancestry, by architects, town planners, and by teachers and schoolchildren involved in local history projects.

In addition, the archive offers every one of us an opportunity to examine the places where we and our families have lived and worked down the years. Highly successful in Frith's own era, the archive is now, a century and more on, entering a new phase of popularity.

## The Past in Tune with the Future

Historians consider the Francis Frith Collection to be of prime national importance. It is the only archive of its kind remaining in private ownership and has been valued at a million pounds. However, this figure is now rapidly increasing as digital technology enables more and more people around the world to enjoy its benefits.

Francis Frith's archive is now housed in an historic timber barn in the beautiful village of Teffont in Wiltshire. Its founder would not recognize the archive office as it is today. In place of the many thousands of dusty boxes containing glass plate negatives and an all-pervading odour of photographic chemicals, there are now ranks of computer screens. He would be amazed to watch his images travelling round the world at unimaginable speeds through network and internet lines.

The archive's future is both bright and exciting. Francis Frith, with his unshakeable belief in making photographs available to the greatest number of people, would undoubtedly approve of what is being done today with his lifetime's work. His photographs, depicting our shared past, are now bringing pleasure and enlightenment to millions around the world a century and more after his death.

# Hastings & St Leonards

When Hastings and St Leonards are approached from the sea, their beauty is obvious. To the west is the broad sweep of Pevensey Bay, famed in history for being the place where William of Normandy landed to subdue Saxon England and capture a crown. The settlement of Pevensey and the modern resort of Bexhill now grace the long sweep of the bay. To the west of Hastings are the great cliffs of Ecclesbourne, named after the eagles that perhaps once lived there; they are the highest headlands on the Sussex coast, spectacular and dramatic, particularly on wild days when the swirling waters of the English Channel crash against them. The three-mile-long sea front of Hastings and St Leonards is almost as impressive as anything that nature has provided. Away from the shoreline, sharp bluffs and deep valleys dominate the now large townscape, beloved of residents and regular ▶

**Hastings, From East Cliff 1891** 29039
The very name of Hastings suggests that most famous date in English history - 1066, though King Harold's defeat at the hands of William of Normandy actually took place several miles away on Senlac Hill, the place known today as Battle. The settlements around the site of present-day Hastings did suffer, though, during William's preliminary skirmishes.

visitors. Hastings' old castle, though now a ruin, still dominates the sea-lanes like some challenging watchdog much as it has done every day for nearly a thousand years.

One date, 1066, fixes Hastings in everyone's consciousness. Yet the famous Battle of Hastings, where Duke William defeated Harold II, was fought several miles away on Senlac Hill; this place was subsequently to take the place name Battle, in awe and tribute to the bloody events of a few hours that changed the course of England's history. This is not to suggest that the place we now know as Hastings played no part in the invasion, for it was from this easily-defended area that William set out to join battle with the English army. Locals still point out a slab of stone close to the pier where William is said to have breakfasted before marching away to Senlac. A more certain reminder is the castle, standing stark and threatening on a hillside above the town. Not long after his victory, William, insecure and with a whole countryside still to quell, built a wooden fortification upon this high bluff. In time, a stone castle replaced it, to warn off other potential invaders.

However, 1066 is just one event in the long and remarkable history of Hastings. Prehistoric dwellers scratched a living amongst the hills and valleys on which the town now stands. Flint implements are sometimes found in local gardens and the downlands nearby. A land bridge connected England to the Continent during the early part of the Stone Age, and the inhabitants of this district would have hunted in long-drowned forests and plains. Remains of trees from this lost landscape have been found along nearby shorelines, and submerged woodland is thought to have stretched across what is now Pevensey Bay. Tree stumps are occasionally found at low tide and after storms.

Even before the arrival of William, the Saxons must have held Hastings in high regard, for King Athelstan established a mint here in 928. Norman and Angevin kings made a point of visiting quite regularly during the first troubled centuries of the Middle Ages. The Conqueror's son William Rufus spent a festive month at the castle in the company of his court and army, awaiting a fair wind to cross to Normandy. And it was here that the unfortunate King John declared England to be the 'Master of the Sea' - a foolish boast, for Hastings, like so many south coast towns, was to suffer repeated French raids in the centuries that followed.

It was in an atmosphere of threats from abroad that Hastings was created one of the five (subsequently seven) Cinque Ports - these were essentially a naval confederacy, designed to defend the shores of England and to keep open the nation's sea-lanes. Henry III decreed that Hastings must provide six ships for the defence of the realm. The fact that Hastings could do so, shows how prosperous the town must have been at this time. To compensate for the burden laid down upon them, the Cinque Ports were exempted from all other military duties, allowed to trade free of toll, and permitted to govern themselves with little outside interference.

The silting of the harbour led to the decline of Hastings as a port. Now even the site has been built upon, and a few house and shop names are the only reminders of the importance of the town's naval and mercantile past. Not that the borough gave in easily to the loss of this important facility. Town records tell of several failed attempts to construct a new harbour, the last - of which a breakwater remains - being in 1893.

Denied the shelter of any sort of port, fishing vessels have in recent times been launched from the beach, and hauled back up the sands using muscle-power and motors. Some of the most evocative photographs in this collection show the Old Town, with the tall and tarred wooden buildings of its picturesque fishermen's quarter, parts of which dated back to Elizabethan times. The fishermen had to pay ground rent, and therefore constructed these extraordinary buildings upwards to keep down costs. The Frith photographs provide a valuable historical record, for a number of the buildings shown here were lost in a devastating fire in 1961.

Hastings finally overcame the loss of its port by becoming a health resort in the late 18th century; the climate was conducive for both summer and winter holidays. Following the example of George III, who sojourned at Weymouth, and his son the Prince Regent, who made the reputation of Brighton, fashionable folk flocked to Hastings, inspired by the much-publicised medical opinions of society doctors. A whole programme of construction began, which continued for much of the next century, as hotels and villas were built to cater for the influx of vacationers. Many of the streets seen in these photographs date back to this building boom. Roads were laid out and cliffs carved away; pleasure grounds and promenades were

designed to entertain the stroller, and excursions were provided to neighbouring beauty spots. The Parade was begun in 1811 by a Mr Barry, anxious to provide a walkway to benefit the subscribers to his lending library, who might have to pass that way on stormy days. Much new building took place to the west of the Old Town, and the new community of St Leonards was founded in 1828. As time went on, the town grew quickly; luxury hotels, boarding houses, churches and residential areas added to the townscape and provided facilities not only for the visitor, but for the rapidly increasing resident population. The Hastings and St Leonards of today is one of England's largest resorts, but the attractive setting has hardly been compromised by its swift growth.

These photographs capture Hastings and St Leonards from the high Victorian age to the 1950s, giving us some idea of how the town developed from an exclusive health resort to a venue for popular seaside holidays. In the seventy years captured here we see bathing fashions change, the dress of promenaders become less modest, and transport develop from horse-drawn carriages through electric trams and charabanc to the arrival of the soon-to-be-ubiquitous motor car. But the beauty and atmosphere of this much-loved and historic holiday resort remains unchanged.

**Hastings**
**The Castle Ruins 1890** 22791
Hastings Castle has a long and eventful history: an
early construction, probably made of wood, was set
in hand soon after William's success in battle. The
ruins we see today are mostly medieval, but the
setting gives some idea of how much importance the
Norman invaders attached to dominating a
troublesome Saxon countryside.

**Hastings, The Castle 1925** 77965
Little remains of the chapel inside the castle of which Thomas Becket was once Dean in the reign of Henry II. The later Collegiate Church of the Blessed Virgin Mary is also just a ruin. The presence of religious buildings within the castle shows the increasing influence of the church during the reigns of the Angevin and Plantagenet kings.

**Hastings, The Castle 1925** 77968
A number of English kings stayed at the castle on their frequent visits to Hastings. William Rufus held court here, at the head of his army, awaiting a chance to slip across to Normandy. In 1201 King John declared the English to be masters of the sea whilst he was here - though he had to reduce the fortifications in 1216 to prevent the castle's capture by the French.

▼ **Hastings, St Clement's Church 1890** 22788

The original parish church stood nearer to the sea, which claimed the building in 1236. Its replacement was destroyed during a French raid in 1378. The present lovely building dates back to around 1380. It was in St Clement's that the artist Dante Gabriel Rossetti married Elizabeth Siddall, the inspiration and model for some of his best work, in 1860.

▼ **Hastings, All Saints' Church 1890** 22790

All Saints' Church, erected in 1436, bears a resemblance to St Clement's in design. The church was occupied briefly by Parliamentary forces during the English Civil War, and later acquired notoriety by having Titus Oates as its curate.

▲ **Hastings Normanhurst 1891**

29044

Many a Victorian visitor to Hastings travelled out of town to view Earl Brassey's imposing mansion of Normanhurst, ten miles to the north-west. The foundation stone of this imposing house was laid in 1865.

◀ **Hastings
Normanhurst 1891** 29043
The building took six years
to complete. Brassey coined
the name Normanhurst to
link together the combatant
sides of the battle of 1066:
Norman, for William's
invaders, and Hurst, the old
Saxon name for a wood.

◄ **Hastings Ecclesbourne Glen Bridge 1890** 25378
This picturesque little ravine, enlivened by the sound of running water, derives its name from the bourne of the eagles. Quite close to Hastings, this beauty spot would have been much visited by Victorian tourists on their way to Fairlight Glen. A little hut provided refreshments for the sustenance of the traveller.

### Hastings, Fairlight Glen Lovers' Seat 1890 25379

Victorians flocked to see the Lovers' Seat in the beauty spot of Fairlight Glen. Tradition alleges that a naval lieutenant called Lamb trysted here with his sweetheart Miss Boys. Their relationship met with family disapproval, hence the secret meeting-place. The pair eventually married at St Clement Danes Church in London in 1786. The original seat was a long rock that tumbled away in a landslide.

### Hastings Alexandra Park 1890

25376

This area was once known at St Andrews Gardens; after the Prince and Princess of Wales, later Edward VII and Queen Alexandra, opened Alexandra Park, the park was later renamed in honour of Princess Alexandra. Its 80 acres comprise woodland, lakes and sports grounds.

### Hastings Alexandra Park 1890

25374

Alexandra Park has long been a popular venue for entertainment, fetes and shows. The lake and reservoir have been stocked with trout and coarse fish for the benefit of local anglers.

**Hastings, East Cliff 1890** 22794
A hydraulic lift transported visitors from sea level up the cliffside to the grassy slopes of East Hill, from where earlier tourists would have walked to Ecclesbourne Glen and Fairlight Glen. Notice the number of shanties at the foot of the cliff.

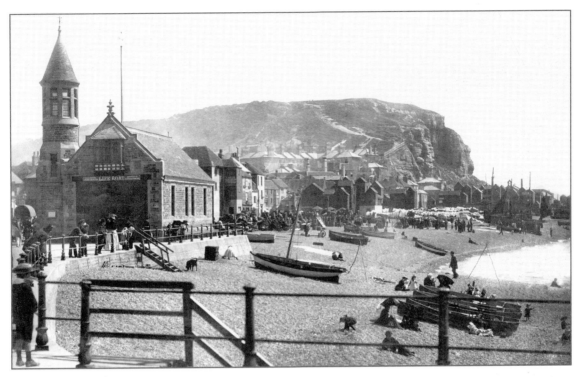

**Hastings, The Lifeboat Station 1890** 22784

The Lifeboat House stands on the site of the original Hastings Custom House, which was washed away by the sea during a gale in 1880. Spectators gathered on stormy days, heedless of the weather, to watch the lifeboat being launched.

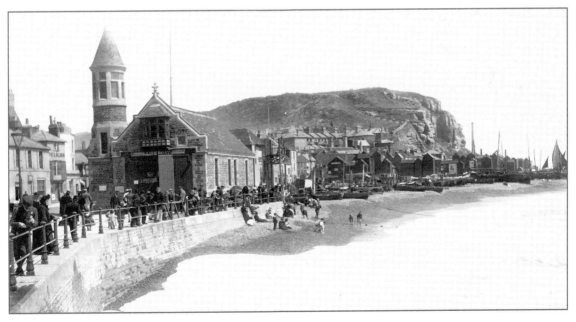

**Hastings, The Lifeboat Station 1894** 34427

**Hastings
The Pier 1890** 22780
Hastings' pier cost
£23,000 when it was
built in 1872. It was
originally some nine
hundred feet long; it
made a dramatic
structure for strolling
along and seeking
seaside entertainments.
The fine pavilion at the
end of the pier was
destroyed by fire
in 1917.

**Hastings, The Sea Front from the Pier 1890** 25351
Hastings has a shingle beach accessed from a promenade of some three miles in length from East Cliff to St Leonards. A long strip of sand is revealed at low tide - rather like neighbouring Bexhill.

**Hastings
The Esplanade 1890**

25353

Bathing machines were used at Hastings until well into the last century, though changing cabins and tents gradually superseded them. Mixed bathing was allowed at the resort from Victorian times.

**Hastings
The Beach 1890** 25357
This wonderful scene of
late Victorian beach
fashion shows perhaps
why mixed bathing was
so easily tolerated -
even the children
having a paddle seem
overdressed by modern
standards. Victorians
who wished to divest
themselves of all this
apparel would seek
isolated beaches below
the clifftops.

◀ **St Leonards
The Pier 1891** 29607
St Leonards Pier opened
in 1891 at an initial cost
of £30,000 as a
companion for the pier
at Hastings. Nearby is
the Conqueror's Stone,
said to have been used
as a table by Duke
William of Normandy
before he marched off
to battle.

### St Leonards
### The Sussex Hotel 1890

25366

St Leonards and Hastings are now effectively just one town, running into each other and controlled by the same local authority. In Victorian times, St Leonards was a separate community; it was only in the 20th century that the green gap between them was bridged by development.

### St Leonards, The Royal
### Victoria Hotel 1891   29608

Hastings and St Leonards quickly acquired a reputation as a resort for both summer and winter. A range of hotels and boarding houses were built to cater for most pockets, including the Royal Victoria, which is an excellent example of period architecture. King Louis Philippe of France lived here in exile after being ousted in the Revolution of 1848.

### Hastings
### The Beach c1890

H36301

Early visitors came to Hastings as much for the benefit to health as pure holiday. The climate is mild at most times of the year, and the hills round and about the town shield bathers from the colder winds. By ascending the clifftops and walking the downs, the bracing effects of the southern English climate could be experienced.

**Hastings, Ecclesbourne Cliffs 1894** 34438
The cliffs of Ecclesbourne, at over six hundred feet, are the highest on the Sussex coast, making for spectacular scenery and exciting walks. These coastal paths would have been used originally by Customs Officers seeking to curb the activities of the notorious local smuggling gangs.

**Hastings, Ecclesbourne Glen 1925** 77991

The nearness of this coast to France meant that it was ideal for smuggling. Many local fishermen in past centuries involved themselves in 'the trade' as a way of supplementing their incomes when times were hard. Even as late as 1831, a smuggling affray at Ecclesbourne led to the deaths of two men.

**Hastings, Ecclesbourne Glen 1925** 77992
Visitors in the 20th century enjoyed the delights of the Glens of Ecclesbourne and Fairlight just as much as their Victorian forebears had. Despite some developments, the coast between Hastings and Rye remains wild and rugged.

**Hastings, The Coast and the Downs 1894** 34436
On wilder winter days, with a storm beating up the Channel, the walk along the cliffs east of Hastings can be an exciting excursion, with salt spray soaking the clifftop rambler and fierce winds making progress difficult.

**Hastings, Fairlight Glen, Dripping Well 1925** 77995
At the time this photograph was taken, charabancs would leave the monument in Hastings each day to visit local beauty spots such as Fairlight Glen. The Glen's Dripping Well was situated just below the famous Lovers' Seat, and was a favourite subject for both artist and photographer.

**Hastings**
**View from the Pier 1925** 77972
In 1913, Hastings Corporation began an ambitious scheme at a
cost of £100,000 to improve all aspects of the sea front - including
the construction of places of entertainment, pleasure grounds and
a bandstand with seating accommodation for two thousand people.

**Hastings, The Pier 1925** 77984

As well as a venue for entertainment, the Pier was used as a landing stage for steamer trips. In good weather, steamers would take tourists on voyages to Dover, Folkestone, Brighton, Eastbourne and the Isle of Wight. Trips along the local coastline were very popular with visitors who had less time on their hands.

**Hastings, The Esplanade 1925** 77976

Just across from the pier is the entrance to the White Rock Baths, part of a leisure complex, with bowling greens and tennis courts. The foundation stone for a new hospital was laid nearby by the Duke of Richmond in 1914.

**Hastings
View from the Pier
1925** 77975
Hastings' proximity to
London made the resort
very popular during the
20th century, as
seaside holidays came
within the budget of a
wider section of the
population. Hastings
and St Leonards
provided a range of
accommodation to suit
every pocket.

**Hastings**
**The Beach 1925**  77979
Despite the silting up of
Hastings' original
harbour, fishermen and
boatmen continued to
ply their trade from this
long strand. With the
advent of tourism, some
boatmen offered local
boat and fishing trips
along the Sussex coast.

**Hastings, The Beach 1925** 77980
On a clear day, Eastbourne may be seen to the west across Pevensey Bay from Hastings Pier and the sea front. To the east are clear views to the broad peninsula of Dungeness.

**Hastings, The Beach 1925** 77983
Very few parts of the town are far from the beach. These visitors in 1925 had the advantage of an electric tramway linking all parts of Hastings and St Leonards - a useful means of transport for those wishing to travel further afield than the sea front.

**Hastings, The Bowling Green 1925**  77985
Hastings has a fine bowling green within a few minutes walk of the sea front. At this time, use of the green cost 4d an hour, though a season ticket could be obtained for £1 5s.

**Hastings
The Bandstand 1925**
77986
Summer season band
performances in the
1920s took place three
times a day. Apart from
local bands, well-known
performance musicians
would travel to Hastings
to entertain the tourists.

▼ **Hastings, Old Town c1955** H36014

Hastings was one of the five ancient Cinque Ports of England, but the eastwards drift of sand and shingle eventually silted up the town's harbour. The site was built upon, and only the names of a few buildings provide evidence of its existence.

▼ **Hastings, Old Town c1955** H36015

Hastings remained an easy place to drive around even as late as the 1950s. However, towards the end of the last century motor traffic proved a problem, and parking became difficult in the town. Here we see a relatively traffic-free sea front.

▲ **Hastings, Old Town c1955** H36017

This is one of the oldest parts of Hastings, much loved by visitors for the excellent bathing beaches nearby, or just as a convenient place for a stroll on a pleasant evening.

**Hastings, The Beach c1955** H36021

▼ **Hastings, The Fishing Quarter c1955** H36001
The Fishermen's Quarter of Hastings is seen here at its picturesque best near the Stade, or landing place. Shipbuilding was once an important industry here, and fish were sold in the local market. A fishermen's church, built in 1854 at a cost of £600, was well used by seafarers before they undertook perilous journeys.

▼ **Hastings, View from the Castle c1955** H36003
Since probably the earliest days of Hastings, people staying in the town have made their way uphill to the castle - at first out of duty, then for pleasure, so as to admire the ancient structure and the extensive views in every direction.

▲ **Hastings, View from the Castle c1955** H36005
Here we have a fine view over part of the old town and breakwater, giving some idea of how well the castle guarded the English Channel during the troubled centuries of strife with France. When kept in good order, the castle was a sufficient obstacle to raids and invasions.

◄ **Hastings, View from the Castle c1955** H36007
This view looks across the West Hill recreation ground, with St Clement's Church in the valley below. The later 20th century brought more development to this area, though the scene could still be recognised by today's observer.

**Hastings, Marine Court c1955** H36029
Though rooted in history, Hastings has never been afraid of change. Newer buildings are now dominating the skyline - such as this restaurant at Marine Court. Some of the old buildings were unfortunately sacrificed, and the modern photographer can never recapture many of the scenes in these photographs.

**Hastings, Warrior Square c1955** H36026
By the mid 1950s, the long period of austerity that had blighted wartime and post-war Britain was coming to an end. The availability of affordable motor cars meant that resorts such as Hastings were given a new lease of life, and tourists arrived in greater numbers than ever before.

**Hastings, The Clock Tower c1955** H36033
This clock tower is a memorial to Prince Albert, Consort of Queen Victoria, and was erected by public subscription in 1862. It stands at the junction of six roads, which has always been a busy place - the extensive electric tramway system radiated out from here in earlier days.

**Hastings, The Sea Front c1955**  H36050
Although the electric trams disappeared in the latter half of the 20th century, Hastings and St Leonards are still easily and best explored using public transport, a bicycle or shanks's pony. These sea front walks are as popular as ever.

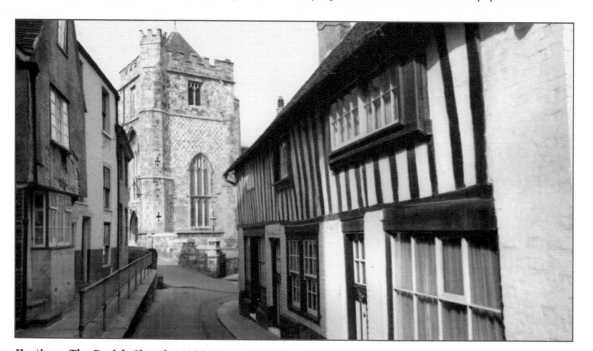

**Hastings, The Parish Church c1955**  H36041
This final glimpse of old Hastings is a photograph that captures all the charms of the old town, with St Clement's Church at the end of the street. After visiting Hastings, the tourist should make the short journey out to Battle to see where the course of English history was changed so suddenly and dramatically on an October day in 1066.

# Bexhill-on-Sea

A couple of centuries ago, a pedestrian walking around the shoreline of Pevensey Bay would have found only a modest inland village amid bare downland and farmed fields where Bexhill-on-Sea stands today; it would have been little changed in outlook from the coastal scenery watched carefully by William the Conqueror as his ships came ashore nearby in 1066. For Bexhill-on-Sea ▶

**Bexhill**
**The Smithy and the Jubilee Clock 1891** 28442
Bexhill really is a resort of the past 120 years, for earlier in Queen Victoria's reign it was scarcely more than a village, set well back from the sea. This first sequence of photographs shows scenes from the older part of the resort - the Old Town. The clock seen here celebrates Victoria's Golden Jubilee of 1887.

is one of England's youngest seaside resorts - the earlier inland site has now sprawled out across the once undisturbed coastline.

In 1881, Bexhill's population was a modest 2000. By 1891, when the first of these Frith photographs was taken, the population had increased to over 5000. By the 1920s, the number of residents had trebled, and the heart of the town resembled the resort that we see today. Initially, people came to Bexhill purely for health reasons: the climate and atmosphere were conducive to a good constitution, with bracing winds, inviting rambles, and plenty of sunshine. The town held a record for a low death rate, sparking the local whimsy that 'a person may live in Bexhill just as long as he chooses'. Influential doctors gave the town a ringing health endorsement; one doctor commented that 'residence at Bexhill is especially beneficial in anaemia, scrofula, and tuberculous diseases, and in diseases of the respiratory organs'. A huge convalescent home was built in 1880, and the fame of Bexhill was established. The opening of the home probably gave the little town all the impetus it needed to develop as a major resort.

The little inland village that an early Victorian wanderer would have seen remains, under the guise of the 'Old Town' and away from the coast and the later resort. This old part of Bexhill dates back at least to Saxon times, for we know that King Offa of Mercia gave a grant of land in 772 so that the parish church might be enlarged. These were troubled times for Sussex's Saxon Shore. In the succeeding centuries, Viking raiders probed the coast, looting and burning the tiny settlements hard by the sea. This threat may explain the reluctance of the early villagers to develop a community nearer to the English Channel.

St Peter's Church stands at the heart of this ancient quarter, much restored since Saxon days, but still a building of considerable antiquity and charm. Building work in 1878 revealed a carved Saxon coffin lid, which was fixed to a wall of the tower for all to see - a reminder of Bexhill's past links to the time of Offa, Alfred and Athelstan. Perhaps we should not call this place Bexhill at all, but Bexelei, the place name recorded in the Domesday Book. The Old Town remains not so very different to the village which was captured as a working community in these early Frith photographs; but inevitably some buildings were lost in the careless days of the 20th century.

For much of the thousand years that followed Domesday, Bexhill remained an isolated farming hamlet, left behind by the more dramatic tides of English history. All was to change with the renewal of threats from the not so distant continent of Europe. To counter a possible invasion by Napoleon Bonaparte, a dozen Martello towers were built along the coastline, and several thousand troops of the King's German Legion were billeted in a purpose-built barracks in the heart of the old village. The presence of a military base changed Bexhill for ever, indirectly leading to the area's development as a resort, for word of its attractions was spread by the soldiers and families based there.

Looking at these photographs of Bexhill-on-Sea, it becomes clear that what we are seeing is very much a purpose-built seaside resort, for the emphasis of almost all of the architecture is on comfort, fun and seaside pleasures. From late Victorian times a great building programme was instigated: parades and promenades were laid out, sports fields and parks opened, venues for entertainment created, and access to the sea improved. At a first glance, the beach was not immediately welcoming, showing more shingle than sand at high tide; though delightful stretches of sand are revealed as the sea flows back. Resorts with this problem tended to do all they could to distract the eye by making the shoreline attractive in other ways - hence the very considerable financial investment in the promenade. Bathing cabins and tents were provided on the edge of the strand to lure bathers on to the beach, and a large swimming pool opened in Egerton Park.

Bexhill was raised to borough status in 1902, a remarkable achievement considering that this had been a humble village of some 500 people only a century earlier. By the beginning of Edward VII's reign, a two-mile-long sea front had been constructed for the benefit of promenaders and cyclists, and accommodation was available to suit every pocket. A new Pavilion, named after local benefactor Earl De La Warr, gave a boost to entertainment in the resort, with band performances, shows and concerts during the season. A direct rail link to the town opened in the year that Bexhill became a borough, bringing increased numbers of tourists and allowing the town to compete on equal terms with longer-established resorts. Many visitors to Bexhill became so enamoured with the place that they decided to settle there permanently, creating a surrounding layer of villas and smart houses, the residential area of Bexhill-on-Sea that we know today.

In our photographic journey around Bexhill we start, quite properly, in the Old Town, the original Bexhill of Saxon times, with its lovely parish church and historic and influential manor house. At the time that the earliest of these photographs was taken, this was still a discrete agricultural community, despite the growth of the newer seaside resort a little distance away. We then follow the fortunes of Bexhill through its elegant Victorian and Edwardian heyday to the carefree days of the 1920s, watching fashions change from the modest and over-dressed seaside promenaders of Victoria's England to the post First World War generation, throwing away their cares in the first decade of peace in lovely Bexhill.

**Bexhill**
**The Manor House Tennis Court 1892** 30462
Bexhill's ancient manor house was a retreat for
the Bishops of Chichester in the Middle Ages,
before passing into the ownership of several
notable English families such as the Dorsets
and Brooks. At the time this photograph was
taken it was in the possession of Viscount
Cantelupe, heir to the Earldom of De La Warr.

**Bexhill**
**The Downs and the Cricket Ground**
**1894** 33847
Before the new resort grew up across the
landscape, much of the countryside
around the old village was open downland
along the breezy coastal strip. As the
resort developed, walkers and horseriders
used the downs for recreation.

**Bexhill**
**The Old Town 1897** 38994
This older part of the original
Bexhill, or rather Bexle, was
Saxon in origin. History records
that in 772 King Offa of Mercia
gave a grant of land to enlarge the
parish church. By the time of
Domesday Book, 'Bexelei' was
recorded as a small village, which
had scarcely recovered from the
Norman invasion.

**Bexhill, The Convalescent Home 1891** 28431
From its first days as a resort, Bexhill gained a reputation as a place beneficial to good health. Medicinal baths were available at the Hydro, and many visitors came for the bracing sea breezes and salt-water bathing. The town has long had one of the lowest death rates in Britain.

**Bexhill, The Convalescent Home 1891** 28433
This striking building is the Metropolitan Convalescent Home, founded in 1880. When this photograph was taken, the building housed both men and women invalids, but in 1905 a separate male institution was opened at Cooden Down.

**Bexhill, The Convalescent Home 1899** 43284
This rare photograph shows the interior of the convalescent home at the end of Queen Victoria's reign. The opening of this home gave the developing town of Bexhill a great boost as a leading health resort.

**Bexhill, The Walnut Tree 1903** 50318
Bexhill's famous walnut tree began life within the manor grounds. Late in Victorian times the road was widened, and the tree became a prominent roadside landmark. The stump was finally removed in 1921. Just by the tree is some photographic equipment, perhaps belonging to the Frith photographer.

**Bexhill**
**The Old Town 1903** 50317
This view looks down Bexhill's original High Street. In the distance is Barrack Hall, occupied by a garrison of troops during the Napoleonic Wars. An advertisement in Mr Ballard's shop on the right promotes footwear by telling us that 'by wearing these boots corns disappear'.

**Bexhill, The Old Town 1912** 64958
Townsfolk gather outside Bexhill's forge in the early years of George V's reign. The forge continued to serve local needs until the 1940s, and was demolished in 1947. The building on the opposite side of the road was taken down two decades later.

**Bexhill, The Old Town, St Peter's Parish Church 1921** 70525
Bexhill's parish church probably started its long history in Saxon times, though it has been restored many times since. In 1878 the carved coffin lid of a Saxon was discovered during renovations and was displayed on the south wall of the church tower.

**Bexhill, The Old Town 1921** 70526
In the line of old shops we can see W H Dann, newsagent, fruiterer and florist; Woolleys, plumbers and electricians; and A Norris, boot maker. The stump of the walnut tree was removed soon after this photograph was taken.

▼ **Bexhill, From the Coastguard Station 1891** 28412
Victorian development turned the focus of the resort away from the
old town and towards the sea front. At this time new hotels and
boarding houses were built, convalescent and recreational facilities
were opened, and the beach was improved for bathing.

▼ **Bexhill, Devonshire Road 1891** 28421
Devonshire Road was one of the first sights of Bexhill for many visitors,
for a railway station existed at one end of the road. Bexhill was
fortunate to boast two railway stations and a couple of halts at around
this time.

▲ **Bexhill, Devonshire
Road 1899** 43279
A walk along Devonshire
Road took the arriving
visitor from the railway
station to the sea front,
passing a number of
shops, offices, small
hotels and boarding
houses along the way.
Devonshire Road boasts a
great deal of functional
Victorian architecture, as
befits a purpose-built
seaside town. This was
very much the business
area of the town.

◀ **Bexhill, Galley Hill Cliffs 1894** 33860
The coastal scenery around Bexhill may not be the most spectacular along the southern coast of England, but it does offer many pleasant walks - beneficial to those who come to the area for health reasons.

◄ **Bexhill, The Cycle Boulevard and the Sackville Hotel 1897**

38984

Cyclists were encouraged to use this specially constructed boulevard on Bexhill's sea front. The building in the distance is the Kursaal, built under the patronage of Earl De La Warr as a place of entertainment. It was officially opened the year before this photograph was taken. The Kursaal had a short life, changing its name to the Pavilion in the early years of the last century. It was demolished in 1936.

### ◀ Bexhill, From Galley Hill 1897   38980

This view looks across the downs towards distant Bexhill, with a pair of golfers practising their sport to the right of the photograph. A formal golf course was opened in 1912 at Cooden, complete with its own railway halt.

### ▼ Bexhill, The Sackville Hotel and the Kiosk 1897   38986

The Sackville Hotel dominates the De La Warr Parade, named after the family who did much to promote Bexhill at this time. The Sackville was one of several first-class hotels built along the sea front in Victorian times.

### ◀ Bexhill The Parade and the Marine Hotel 1899   43216

The coming of the railway made the development of a modern resort possible. The Parade was one of the first areas to be built, with a straight line of Victorian properties all along the sea front - many of which have survived into this century.

**Bexhill
The Parade 1897**
38989
This parade was named after the 7th earl De La Warr, who died in 1896. His son, the 8th earl, devoted much of his time to the affairs of the town, including serving a spell as Chairman of the council. He died in Sicily in 1915, having just returned from the Dardanelles battlefield.

**Bexhill, De La Warr Parade 1899** 43219
A great variety of accommodation was offered to visitors to Bexhill, from modest boarding houses to grand hotels. The move away from the vicinity of Old Town to the coastal strip meant that the majority of these were built within a short walk of the beach.

▼ **Bexhill, De La Warr Parade and the Bandstand 1899** 43221
Band performances were held mostly at the Colonnade after it was
opened in 1911. Popular tunes of the day were played by resident and
visiting bands to amuse the visitors, who lounged in the surrounding
deckchairs. On Sundays there would be a programme of sacred music.

▼ **Bexhill, The Lane Monument 1899** 43227
This monument in Town Hall Square commemorates Lt Col Henry Lane, the
distinguished soldier and veteran of the Indian Mutiny. Lane was a notable Justice
of the Peace and eventual Chairman of Bexhill Urban District Council. Lane was
Bexhill's first county alderman until his death in 1896.

▲ **Bexhill
The Parade 1903** 50305
Before 1902, Bexhill was
governed by an Urban
District Council. However,
with the rapid growth of
the resort, it acquired
borough status; its area
extended from Pevensey
Sluice to Bulverhythe.

**Bexhill, The Kursaal 1903** 50306
The Duchess of Teck, mother of the future Queen Mary, opened the Kursaal in 1896. These ornamental gates could be closed to prevent traffic entering the Parade, a useful function in the early days of motor cars. The poster by the pillar advertises a performance of 'The Mikado'.

◄ **Bexhill
Sea Road 1903** 50314
Sea Road is the direct route between the Old Town and the newer resort of Bexhill. One of the town's original railway stations was easily accessible from this busy thoroughfare.

### ◀ Bexhill
### The Parade 1903 50308

Motor cars were still a novelty in and around Bexhill in 1903, though a variety of other methods of transport were being used. Visitors could use the train to neighbouring places of interest, where they could explore the locality on foot or bicycle. Younger tourists could perhaps sample donkey rides or carts drawn by an agreeable goat.

### Bexhill, The Clock ▶
### Tower and the
### Bandstand 1904 52895

This attractive clock tower on West Parade was, as the inscription states, 'erected by the Council and inhabitants of Bexhill to commemorate the Coronation of His Majesty King Edward VII, on the 9th August, 1902'.

### ◀ Bexhill, West Parade
### 1904 52893

Children play with hoops on Bexhill's West Parade, that lovely sweeping 800-yard-long promenade and carriage drive. West Parade had to be repaired several times in the last century after being damaged by gales. This unusually designed bandstand finally succumbed to the power of the sea in the 1960s.

**Bexhill, The Parade
1910** 62925
Wearing broad hats or
carrying parasols to
protect complexions
from the rays of the sun,
these promenaders
amble along Bexhill's sea
front during the last year
of King Edward's reign.

▼ **Bexhill, Central Parade 1910** 62931
The Colonnade was opened as a place for popular entertainments
and promenading in 1911 at a cost of £4000. The cliff was cut back
to form a semi-circular gallery, which could be closed off on the
seaward side during bad weather.

▼ **Bexhill, The Bandstand 1912** 64949
Many excellent bands and orchestras entertained holidaymakers at
Bexhill during the height of the season, either at the Colonnade or at
other locations around the resort. How delightful it must have been to
hear your favourite music as you bathed in the sea.

▲ **Bexhill
The Beach 1910** 62937
At low tide, the sands of
Bexhill beach are fully
revealed for bathing,
shrimping and sandcastle
building expeditions. At
high tide the beach is
much shinglier, for the
sands are only revealed
when the sea is out.
Some early visitors who
saw only the shingle fled
to other resorts, thinking
Bexhill unsuitable for
beach activities.

◄ **Bexhill
The Beach 1912** 64954
A row of bathing tents lines the long strip of shingle at the head of Bexhill's beach. Bexhill was one of the first Victorian resorts to allow mixed bathing. Early guidebook writers advised bathers to wear shoes for the walk across the shingle to the sand when the tide was right out.

◄ **Bexhill
De La Warr Parade
1921** 70523
In the 1920s, Bexhill still attracted the invalid and the valetudinarian. One medical expert at the time boasted that 'residence at Bexhill is especially beneficial in anaemia, scrofula and tuberculous diseases, and in diseases of the respiratory organs'.

◀ **Bexhill**
**The Parade 1912**
64946
This area has changed somewhat since this view was taken in the early years of George V's reign. The ornamental gates have been removed, and some of these imposing buildings demolished. The Kursaal, on the left of the photograph, is no more.

▼ **Bexhill**
**De La Warr Parade 1921** 70520
Though never a great centre for water sports, Bexhill boasts a yacht club, and sea anglers may often be seen casting their lines from the beach or promenade.

◀ **Bexhill**
**The Marina 1927**
79698
This view of the sea front shows how clear was the divide between wheeled transport and pedestrians. One of the advantages of constructing a new town was that the designers were not bound to follow the line of narrow ancient highways; thus a great deal of space for promenading was provided.

**Bexhill
The Marina 1921**
70514
A charabanc and its driver wait for passengers to arrive on a quiet day in 1921. In the lower right-hand corner of the photograph is an invalid ex-serviceman - perhaps a survivor of the recent First World War.

**Bexhill**
**Egerton Park 1927** 79707
A couple of minutes' walk from the beach is the
lovely open space of Egerton Park. When this view
was taken in 1927, the park could boast an
ornamental lake, a pergola for entertainments, lawns
for tennis, bowls and croquet, a swimming pool
and the town museum.

**Crowhurst**
**The Yew Tree 1907** 57235
A favourite excursion for visitors from both Bexhill
and Hastings was to the famous yew tree at nearby
Crowhurst. The tree is reputedly over three thousand
years old - older than both resorts, and ancient even
when William the Conqueror landed
at Pevensey in 1066.

# Index

# Frith Book Co Titles

## www.frithbook.co.uk

The Frith Book Company publishes over 100 new titles each year. A selection of those currently available are listed below. For latest catalogue please contact Frith Book Co.

Town Books 96pp, 100 photos. County and Themed Books 128pp, 150 photos (unless specified). All titles hardback laminated case and jacket except those indicated pb (paperback)

| | | | | | | |
|---|---|---|---|---|---|---|
| Around Bakewell | 1-85937-113-2 | £12.99 | | Exmoor | 1-85937-132-9 | £14.99 |
| Around Barnstaple | 1-85937-084-5 | £12.99 | | Around Falmouth | 1-85937-066-7 | £12.99 |
| Around Bath | 1-85937-097-7 | £12.99 | | Glasgow (pb) | 1-85937-190-6 | £9.99 |
| Berkshire (pb) | 1-85937-191-4 | £9.99 | | Around Great Yarmouth | 1-85937-085-3 | £12.99 |
| Around Blackpool | 1-85937-049-7 | £12.99 | | Around Guildford | 1-85937-117-5 | £12.99 |
| Around Bognor Regis | 1-85937-055-1 | £12.99 | | Hampshire | 1-85937-064-0 | £14.99 |
| Around Bournemouth | 1-85937-067-5 | £12.99 | | Around Harrogate | 1-85937-112-4 | £12.99 |
| Brighton (pb) | 1-85937-192-2 | £8.99 | | Hertfordshire (pb) | 1-85937-247-3 | £9.99 |
| British Life A Century Ago | 1-85937-103-5 | £17.99 | | Around Horsham | 1-85937-127-2 | £12.99 |
| Buckinghamshire (pb) | 1-85937-200-7 | £9.99 | | Around Ipswich | 1-85937-133-7 | £12.99 |
| Around Cambridge | 1-85937-092-6 | £12.99 | | Ireland (pb) | 1-85937-181-7 | £9.99 |
| Cambridgeshire | 1-85937-086-1 | £14.99 | | Isle of Man | 1-85937-065-9 | £14.99 |
| Canals and Waterways | 1-85937-129-9 | £17.99 | | Isle of Wight | 1-85937-114-0 | £14.99 |
| Cheshire | 1-85937-045-4 | £14.99 | | Kent (pb) | 1-85937-189-2 | £9.99 |
| Around Chester | 1-85937-090-x | £12.99 | | Around Leicester | 1-85937-073-x | £12.99 |
| Around Chichester | 1-85937-089-6 | £12.99 | | Leicestershire (pb) | 1-85937-185-x | £9.99 |
| Churches of Berkshire | 1-85937-170-1 | £17.99 | | Around Lincoln | 1-85937-111-6 | £12.99 |
| Churches of Dorset | 1-85937-172-8 | £17.99 | | Lincolnshire | 1-85937-135-3 | £14.99 |
| Colchester (pb) | 1-85937-188-4 | £8.99 | | London (pb) | 1-85937-183-3 | £9.99 |
| Cornwall | 1-85937-054-3 | £14.99 | | Around Maidstone | 1-85937-056-x | £12.99 |
| Croydon Living Memories (pb) | | | | New Forest | 1-85937-128-0 | £14.99 |
| | 1-85937-162-0 | £9.99 | | Around Newark | 1-85937-105-1 | £12.99 |
| Cumbria | 1-85937-101-9 | £14.99 | | Around Newquay | 1-85937-140-x | £12.99 |
| Dartmoor | 1-85937-145-0 | £14.99 | | North Devon Coast | 1-85937-146-9 | £14.99 |
| Around Derby | 1-85937-046-2 | £12.99 | | North London | 1-85937-206-6 | £14.99 |
| Derbyshire (pb) | 1-85937-196-5 | £9.99 | | Northumberland and Tyne & Wear | | |
| Devon | 1-85937-052-7 | £14.99 | | | 1-85937-072-1 | £14.99 |
| Dorset | 1-85937-075-6 | £14.99 | | Norwich (pb) | 1-85937-194-9 | £8.99 |
| Dorset Coast | 1-85937-062-4 | £14.99 | | Around Nottingham | 1-85937-060-8 | £12.99 |
| Down the Severn | 1-85937-118-3 | £14.99 | | Nottinghamshire (pb) | 1-85937-187-6 | £9.99 |
| Down the Thames | 1-85937-121-3 | £14.99 | | Around Oxford | 1-85937-096-9 | £12.99 |
| Around Dublin | 1-85937-058-6 | £12.99 | | Oxfordshire | 1-85937-076-4 | £14.99 |
| East Sussex | 1-85937-130-2 | £14.99 | | Peak District | 1-85937-100-0 | £14.99 |
| Around Eastbourne | 1-85937-061-6 | £12.99 | | Around Penzance | 1-85937-069-1 | £12.99 |
| Edinburgh (pb) | 1-85937-193-0 | £8.99 | | Around Plymouth | 1-85937-119-1 | £12.99 |
| English Castles | 1-85937-078-0 | £14.99 | | Around St Ives | 1-85937-068-3 | £12.99 |
| Essex | 1-85937-082-9 | £14.99 | | Around Scarborough | 1-85937-104-3 | £12.99 |
| Around Exeter | 1-85937-126-4 | £12.99 | | Scotland (pb) | 1-85937-182-5 | £9.99 |

## Available from your local bookshop or from the publisher

# Frith Book Co Titles (continued)

| | | | | | | |
|---|---|---|---|---|---|---|
| Scottish Castles | 1-85937-077-2 | £14.99 | | Around Torbay | 1-85937-063-2 | £12.99 |
| Around Sevenoaks and Tonbridge | 1-85937-057-8 | £12.99 | | Around Truro | 1-85937-147-7 | £12.99 |
| Around Southampton | 1-85937-088-8 | £12.99 | | Victorian & Edwardian Kent | 1-85937-149-3 | £14.99 |
| Around Southport | 1-85937-106-x | £12.99 | | Victorian & Edwardian Maritime Album | | |
| Around Shrewsbury | 1-85937-110-8 | £12.99 | | | 1-85937-144-2 | £17.99 |
| Shropshire | 1-85937-083-7 | £14.99 | | Victorian & Edwardian Yorkshire | 1-85937-154-x | £14.99 |
| South Devon Coast | 1-85937-107-8 | £14.99 | | Victorian Seaside | 1-85937-159-0 | £17.99 |
| South Devon Living Memories | 1-85937-168-x | £14.99 | | Warwickshire (pb) | 1-85937-203-1 | £9.99 |
| Staffordshire (96pp) | 1-85937-047-0 | £12.99 | | Welsh Castles | 1-85937-120-5 | £14.99 |
| Stone Circles & Ancient Monuments | | | | West Midlands | 1-85937-109-4 | £14.99 |
| | 1-85937-143-4 | £17.99 | | West Sussex | 1-85937-148-5 | £14.99 |
| Around Stratford upon Avon | 1-85937-098-5 | £12.99 | | Wiltshire | 1-85937-053-5 | £14.99 |
| Sussex (pb) | 1-85937-184-1 | £9.99 | | Around Winchester | 1-85937-139-6 | £12.99 |

# Frith Book Co titles available Autumn 2000

| | | | | | | | | |
|---|---|---|---|---|---|---|---|---|
| Cotswolds (pb) | 1-85937-230-9 | £9.99 | Sep | | English Country Houses | 1-85937-161-2 | £17.99 | Oct |
| Cornish Coast | 1-85937-163-9 | £14.99 | Sep | | Folkestone (pb) | 1-85937-124-8 | £9.99 | Oct |
| County Durham | 1-85937-123-x | £14.99 | Sep | | Humberside | 1-85937-215-5 | £14.99 | Oct |
| Dorset Living Memories | 1-85937-210-4 | £14.99 | Sep | | Manchester (pb) | 1-85937-198-1 | £9.99 | Oct |
| Dublin (pb) | 1-85937-231-7 | £9.99 | Sep | | Norfolk Living Memories | 1-85937-217-1 | £14.99 | Oct |
| Herefordshire | 1-85937-174-4 | £14.99 | Sep | | Preston (pb) | 1-85937-212-0 | £9.99 | Oct |
| Kent Living Memories | 1-85937-125-6 | £14.99 | Sep | | Reading (pb) | 1-85937-238-4 | £9.99 | Oct |
| Leeds (pb) | 1-85937-202-3 | £9.99 | Sep | | Salisbury (pb) | 1-85937-239-2 | £9.99 | Oct |
| Ludlow (pb) | 1-85937-176-0 | £9.99 | Sep | | South Hams | 1-85937-220-1 | £14.99 | Oct |
| Norfolk (pb) | 1-85937-195-7 | £9.99 | Sep | | Suffolk (pb) | 1-85937-221-x | £9.99 | Oct |
| North Yorks (pb) | 1-85937-236-8 | £9.99 | Sep | | Swansea (pb) | 1-85937-167-1 | £9.99 | Oct |
| Somerset | 1-85937-153-1 | £14.99 | Sep | | West Yorkshire (pb) | 1-85937-201-5 | £9.99 | Oct |
| Surrey (pb) | 1-85937-240-6 | £9.99 | Sep | | | | | |
| Tees Valley & Cleveland | 1-85937-211-2 | £14.99 | Sep | | Around Aylesbury (pb) | 1-85937-227-9 | £9.99 | Nov |
| Thanet (pb) | 1-85937-116-7 | £9.99 | Sep | | Around Bradford (pb) | 1-85937-204-x | £9.99 | Nov |
| Tiverton (pb) | 1-85937-178-7 | £9.99 | Sep | | Around Chichester (pb) | 1-85937-228-7 | £9.99 | Nov |
| Victorian and Edwardian Sussex | | | | | East Anglia (pb) | 1-85937-265-1 | £9.99 | Nov |
| | 1-85937-157-4 | £14.99 | Sep | | East London | 1-85937-080-2 | £14.99 | Nov |
| Weymouth (pb) | 1-85937-209-0 | £9.99 | Sep | | Gloucestershire | 1-85937-102-7 | £14.99 | Nov |
| Worcestershire | 1-85937-152-3 | £14.99 | Sep | | Greater Manchester (pb) | 1-85937-266-x | £9.99 | Nov |
| Yorkshire Living Memories | 1-85937-166-3 | £14.99 | Sep | | Hastings & Bexhill (pb) | 1-85937-131-0 | £9.99 | Nov |
| | | | | | Helston (pb) | 1-85937-214-7 | £9.99 | Nov |
| British Life A Century Ago (pb) | | | | | Lancaster, Morecombe & Heysham (pb) | | | |
| | 1-85937-213-9 | £9.99 | Oct | | | 1-85937-233-3 | £9.99 | Nov |
| Camberley (pb) | 1-85937-222-8 | £9.99 | Oct | | Peterborough (pb) | 1-85937-219-8 | £9.99 | Nov |
| Cardiff (pb) | 1-85937-093-4 | £9.99 | Oct | | Piers | 1-85937-237-6 | £17.99 | Nov |
| Carmarthenshire | 1-85937-216-3 | £14.99 | Oct | | Wiltshire Living Memories | 1-85937-245-7 | £14.99 | Nov |
| Cheltenham (pb) | 1-85937-095-0 | £9.99 | Oct | | Windmills & Watermills | 1-85937-242-2 | £17.99 | Nov |
| Cornwall (pb) | 1-85937-229-5 | £9.99 | Oct | | York (pb) | 1-85937-199-x | £9.99 | Nov |

# See Frith books on the internet www.frithbook.co.uk

# FRITH PRODUCTS & SERVICES

Francis Frith would doubtless be pleased to know that the pioneering publishing venture he started in 1860 still continues today. A hundred and forty years later, The Francis Frith Collection continues in the same innovative tradition and is now one of the foremost publishers of vintage photographs in the world. Some of the current activities include:

## Interior Decoration

Today Frith's photographs can be seen framed and as giant wall murals in thousands of pubs, restaurants, hotels, banks, retail stores and other public buildings throughout the country. In every case they enhance the unique local atmosphere of the places they depict and provide reminders of gentler days in an increasingly busy and frenetic world.

## Product Promotions

Frith products are used by many major companies to promote the sales of their own products or to reinforce their own history and heritage. Frith promotions have been used by Hovis bread, Courage beers, Scots Porage Oats, Colman's mustard, Cadbury's foods, Mellow Birds coffee, Dunhill pipe tobacco, Guinness, and Bulmer's Cider.

## Genealogy and Family History

As the interest in family history and roots grows world-wide, more and more people are turning to Frith's photographs of Great Britain for images of the towns, villages and streets where their ancestors lived; and, of course, photographs of the churches and chapels where their ancestors were christened, married and buried are an essential part of every genealogy tree and family album.

## Frith Products

All Frith photographs are available Framed or just as Mounted Prints and Posters (size 23 x 16 inches). These may be ordered from the address below. From time to time other products - Address Books, Calendars, Table Mats, etc - are available.

## The Internet

Already twenty thousand Frith photographs can be viewed and purchased on the internet. By the end of the year 2000 some 60,000 Frith photographs will be available on the internet. The number of sites is constantly expanding, each focussing on different products and services from the Collection.
The main Frith sites are listed below.
www.francisfrith.co.uk
www.frithbook.co.uk

**See the complete list of Frith Books at:**

*www.frithbook.co.uk*

This web site is regularly updated with the latest list of publications from the Frith Book Company. If you wish to buy books relating to another part of the country that your local bookshop does not stock, you may purchase on-line.

---

*For further information, trade, or author enquiries please contact us at the address below:*
**The Francis Frith Collection, Frith's Barn, Teffont, Salisbury, Wiltshire, England SP3 5QP.**
Tel: +44 (0)1722 716 376  Fax: +44 (0)1722 716 881   Email: uksales@francisfrith.com

# See Frith books on the internet www.frithbook.co.uk

# TO RECEIVE YOUR FREE MOUNTED PRINT

**Mounted Print**
*Overall size 14 x 11 inches*

*Cut out this Voucher and return it with your remittance for £1.50 to cover postage and handling, to UK addresses. For overseas addresses please include £4.00 post and handling. Choose any photograph included in this book. Your SEPIA print will be A4 in size, and mounted in a cream mount with burgundy rule lines, overall size 14 x 11 inches.*

## Order additional Mounted Prints at HALF PRICE (only £7.49 each*)

If there are further pictures you would like to order, possibly as gifts for friends and family, purchase them at half price (no additional postage and handling required).

## Have your Mounted Prints framed*

For an additional £14.95 per print you can have your chosen Mounted Print framed in an elegant polished wood and gilt moulding, overall size 16 x 13 inches (no additional postage and handling required).

---

**\* IMPORTANT!**
These special prices are only available if ordered using the original voucher on this page (no copies permitted) and at the same time as your free Mounted Print, for delivery to the same address

---

## Frith Collectors' Guild

*From time to time we publish a magazine of news and stories about Frith photographs and further special offers of Frith products. If you would like 12 months FREE membership, please return this form.*

*Send completed forms to:*
**The Francis Frith Collection, Frith's Barn, Teffont, Salisbury, Wiltshire SP3 5QP**

---

# *Voucher* for **FREE** and Reduced Price Frith Prints

| Picture no. | Page number | Qty | Mounted @ £7.49 | Framed + £14.95 | Total Cost |
|---|---|---|---|---|---|
| | | 1 | **Free of charge*** | £ | £ |
| | | | £7.49 | £ | £ |
| | | | £7.49 | £ | £ |
| | | | £7.49 | £ | £ |
| | | | £7.49 | £ | £ |
| | | | £7.49 | £ | £ |

| | | |
|---|---|---|
| *Please allow 28 days for delivery* | **\* Post & handling** | **£1.50** |
| **Book Title** . . . . . . . . . . . . . . . | **Total Order Cost** | **£** |

***Please do not photocopy this voucher. Only the original is valid, so please cut it out and return it to us.***

I enclose a cheque / postal order for £ . . . . . . . . . .
made payable to 'The Francis Frith Collection'
OR please debit my Mastercard / Visa / Switch / Amex card
*(credit cards please on all overseas orders)*

Number . . . . . . . . . . . . . . . . . . . . . . . . . . . . . .

Issue No(Switch only) . . . . . . . .Valid from (Amex/Switch) . . . . . . .

Expires . . . . . . . . . . Signature . . . . . . . . . . . . . . . . .

Name Mr/Mrs/Ms . . . . . . . . . . . . . . . . . . . . . . . . . . .

Address . . . . . . . . . . . . . . . . . . . . . . . . . . . . . . . . . .

. . . . . . . . . . . . . . . . . . . . . . . . . . . . . . . . . . . . . . . .

. . . . . . . . . . . . . . . . . . . . . . Postcode . . . . . . . . . . . . . . . .

Daytime Tel No . . . . . . . . . . . . . . . . . . . . .    Valid to 31/12/02

---

# The Francis Frith Collectors' Guild

Please enrol me as a member for 12 months free of charge.

Name Mr/Mrs/Ms . . . . . . . . . . . . . . . . . . . . . . . . . . . . . . . . . .

Address . . . . . . . . . . . . . . . . . . . . . . . . . . . . . . . . . . . . . . . .

. . . . . . . . . . . . . . . . . . . . . . . . . . . . . . . . . . . . . . . . . . . . . .

. . . . . . . . . . . . . . . . . . . . . . . Postcode . . . . . . . . . . . . . . . .

Free Print - see overleaf